AF375497

Tommy's Dinosaur Dig

Tommy's Dinosaur Dig

Angela Hart Aldridge

AHARTBOOKS

Tommy's Dinosaur Dig

Tommy, Lily, Grace, and Ben, four friends bold,
With a shared love for dinosaurs, stories untold.
In a field filled with dirt, rocks, and sand,
They embarked on a journey, hand in hand.

With shovels and pails, they dug in the ground,
Seeking fossils and bones, treasures they found.
Their laughter echoed as they dug with glee,
Imagining the world of the ancient, wild, and free.

One sunny morning, their adventure took flight,
As they ventured forth, hearts shining bright.
Through layers of earth, they dug deep and wide,
In search of ancient creatures, long since tied.

Their dreams took flight like a soaring bird,
As they unearthed mysteries, each one heard.
A stegosaurus friend led them on their way,
To an ancient land where dinosaurs still play.

    T-Rex bones, massive and grand,
Triceratops horns, buried in the sand.
Through jungles and caves, they roamed without fear,
Their friendship growing stronger with each frontier.

In a hidden cave, treasures did gleam,
Sparkling crystals and gems, like a dream.
As the sun dipped low in the sky's embrace,
They rested, memories etched on their face.

Their dreams that night were filled with delight,
In the land of dinosaurs, where everything's right.
For in their hearts, they knew they'd always be,
Exploring together, forever free.

With the dawn's first light, their journey did end,
But their friendship and memories, they'd always defend.
So, like Tommy and friends, remember the tale,
Of courage and friendship that'll never pale.

The End.